THE BOOK
OF DAVID

a coming of age tale

LOLA E. PETERS

Front cover design by Anne Moya
Back cover by Lola E. Peters
Image of Lola E. Peters by Inye Wokoma, Ijo Arts Media Group, Seattle, WA

Dedication

inspire:

Middle English enspire, from Old French inspirer, from Latin inspirare 'breathe or blow into,' from in- 'into' + spirare 'breathe.' The word was originally used of a divine or supernatural being, in the sense 'impart a truth or idea to someone.'

for David:*

    Thank you, for breathing life into a withering spirit and bringing warmth and firelight into the shadows of my soul. May Life return the favor in your own journey.

for Jonathan:*

    May you someday find the love that the man in you deserves.

◈ ◈ ◈ ◈ ◈

Acknowledgements

Deep and abiding gratitude to Niela Miller, Jan Levy, Nikki DeCaires, Karen Toering, Anne Steyh, Rajaa Gharbi, Denise Gantt and Monique Franklin for their support and friendship, and especially for not laughing at me (at least in front of my face... well... not often anyway).

Respect and appreciation for my fellow Cederberg Tea House writers: Jason Lovato, Frank Spaulding, Alexy Damov, and Daniel Clark, as well as Dr. Georgia S. McDade and Seattle's African American Writers' Alliance. Thanks for tolerating my trip down the rabbit hole. And for laughing with/at me.

Blessings to The Royal Room, their bartenders and waitstaff who patiently indulged my Monday night blueberry tea ritual.

Most of all, thanks to "David" and his successor "Jonathan" who taught me that you're never too old to be surprised.

*David and Jonathan are pseudonyms created to protect the less-than-innocent.

Table of Contents

The Fallows

I awoke this morning with the icy fingers of winter
wrapped around my heart.
Slowly, methodically, I searched:
     The Valley of Childhood Loneliness was quiet;
     Disappointment River ran placidly through
          the Peaks of Unrequited Love
     The Sands of Memory seeped methodically through Time.

Yet somewhere, somehow, a frigid mist has crept
     Past forty years of therapeutic ramparts
     Over moats of slain psychological dragons
     Under watchful guard posts: mystical, spiritual, religious
     (OK, the latter were broken down and rusted out years ago)
     Around the third eye, the hippocampus,
          the hairs on the back of my neck.

How, when, where...
no...
Why
has this disquiet interrupted my fallow mind?
Is it seed breaking new ground;
or an arrow slung from an unexpected bow?
Prescience;
or Fear?

I'll just wrap this blanket a bit closer
Go back to sleep
And hope to wake in spring.

Bar Seen

All the pretty ponies
Lined up at the bar
All the hungry wolverines
Staring from afar

Darting eyes scanning
Ready for a meal
Touch-starved bodies yearning
Wanting just to feel

Love will not be found here
Only fear's caress
Nights that end enveloped
In confirmed loneliness.

Food for Thought

Masquerades and peek-a-boo are young girls' games;
Teasing without consequence or expectation.
I am a grown woman
With no time for boys
Who dangle themselves in front of me
Like rabbits before a leopard
Then run off for their mommies
The moment I pounce.

A woman's gotta eat.

2:00am

Chorus:
Somewhere in the world
A man lies curled in his lover's embrace
Somewhere in the world
A child has wonder playing 'cross her face
And somewhere in this open ocean we call life
Somewhere in the day/night mists
There's a glimmering shadow
Calling me.
Somewhere.

Verse 1:
Whose whisper do I follow
That keeps me on this search
And urges me toward hope and not despair?
When I am past aloneness
Into the silent dark
What siren-song compels me ever onward?

Verse 2:
Is anybody out there,
Or is this just a dream
A hide-and-seek concoction of my mind?
The yearning that has led me
To the place where I now stand,
Was it your call
Or just an echo of my aching lonely cry?

Contemplated Love

In the peaceless hunger of a lonely night
I begged the moon for love:

Bring me, I cried,
Someone to make me Dream again,
Think again,
Wish again,
Hope again.

The universe spun and whirled
I turned
And there you were.
And there was I.

What did your heart cry that dreamless night
That brought you me?

After the Fall

Lightning struck
And split me open
To that sweet spot
Where twinkling stars, rainbows, and memories of unicorns reside
Creating an avalanche of glitter and fireworks' sparks
Cascading through my neural network
Erasing every word from my vocabulary
'Til all I could say was
"It's so nice to see you again."
And fear his touch would set me ablaze
A signal fire
For all the world to know
Jericho was conquered.

A Fine Poem

Your eyes sing to me like waves of the ocean
they smile with a knowing of rivers set free
like rapids that challenge the pulse of my heartstrings
a pounding resounding through cavities of my soul
time erased
hearth rekindled
all that's missing is the hot chocolate.

Life After Death

In one breath
One shudder
My life slipped from my lips to yours
One soft moment
Suspended in time
Forever

Moonlight

The wolf sings to his moon
As drops of quicksilver mercury shimmer in the night sky
And frost touches our cheeks

Do you know how beautiful you are by moonlight?

King of Wands, Ice afire
Stirring within me
Hope for nights to come.

The Princess Waits

What if the princess
Actually built the fortress castle
Herself

The moat
    Carrying all her emotions
    Crossable only by a bridge
    Thinly woven from strands of time
    Fastened to the shores of dual realities:
    Past and future; here and now;
    By ancient memories and hope?

The many changing chambers
    Reflecting mirrored terrors:
    Internal and external;
    Revolving, self-renewing,
    Gnawing, pulsing
    Waiting to be vanquished?

The fiery dragon
    Standing at the final guard
    Behind spiked security rails
    Pacing vigilantly without rest
    Daring anyone to approach
    Spewing self-protective rage?

What if the princess
Just wants a prince
Who can defeat the echo of his own fears?

Just... what if...?

A Test of Time

So if the princess is 20 when she bites the apple
and the prince's kiss wakes her 40 years later
is she technically still 20
and can she still run off with the 20-yr old prince
without feeling pervy
or bearing the judgmental wrath
of the ugly step-sisters on the block?

And what of the princess' dream world,
    architecture of her imposed isolation:
    slaying her own dragons
    building her castle brick on brick
    eating fruit born
    from the seeds of her memories
    and carried on winds of hope
    easing at last
    into the comfort of seclusion?

What now of the prince:
    who has awoken not the princess
    of his childhood dreams
    but a queen of her own realm
    driven anew by unfulfilled passions
    beyond his understanding, capacity,
    endurance or will to satisfy?

What yet of the Maiden in the realm
    who frolicked through the meadow
    hoping for just a minute
    glance from the future king
    and groomed her spirit
    to please his eyes alone?

What then of our definition
of possibility
of Hope
of destiny
of Life.
What then of the past perfect future?
What then of this foolishness
Called love?

Springtime Knocks

Tell me not to love Spring
Ignore the lilting call and response
Among robins and budgies outside my office window
Be blind to the dance of pink cherry blossom buds
Straining against the aluminum gray Northwest sky

Remind me that I am not a romantic
Mewing over soft and gooey poems
Written by touchy-feely dreamers
Forgetting the wintered heart
Iced by he-who-shall-not-be-named

Please
Tell me not to love Spring
Oh, and bring iced tea.

One Step At a Time

Two cats wandered through my garden
(pawsteps quiet through the dawn)
Watching chirping breakfast robins
Circling 'round the hedge-rimmed lawn.

As they broke into the clearing,
Grey from east and Rust from west,
I was sure there'd be a contest
To establish who was best.

Backs humped high in watchful caution,
(tails straight, hair standing-on-end)
They approached each other slowly
Listening, sniffing; foe or friend?

Would they come to trust each other?
Would they drop their guards or fight?
Could they learn to share the garden
With its wonders and delights?

As I stared out of my window
In my post-dream reverie,
It was not two cats I saw there,
Rust was you and Grey was me.

Solace
Based on the collage by Diane S. Bradley

Her memory reached him
through time and space
re-igniting synaptic childhood memories
of lost games, failed tests
schoolyard scuffles, romances adrift;
Reminding him
that love
stood steadfastly nearby
to shine a light
on the path
from grief to peace.

11

Individuals
Standing side by side
Adding value to each other
Yet having substance alone.

The perfect twosome.

Remember Time

Remember the days when love
streamed like so much sunshine
it was everywhere you looked
and you couldn't help but get some all over you?

Remember the nights when music
was our heartbeat
keeping us awake, alert, alive
with a sure knowledge it would all be there Forever?

Remember the sunsets
filled with shared sighs, soft laughter,
and tender fingertips
in slow motion until the sun dripped into the sea?

It seemed so easy to live
in wonder, adventure, satisfaction
and feed on expectations, plans
that would come to pass... someday.

Did anyone tell us the hourglass sand
would take so much with it?

He asks me about love

How do you know?
What does it do?
Where does it take you?

I am an elder and
he thinks
I should have answers

So I take him down
The rabbit hole of my life
Laying bare the paths
Taken and not
Barren and fruitful
Illuminating the dead ends
Tugging at pieces of my soul
Still stuck on barbs
Wading through
Brackish pools of
Heartbreak and bubbling wails
Feeding gardens of
Blooming hope
And juice-filled passion
Through deserts
Lifeless and thorny
Drag marks still visible

This is love, he asks.

I don't know
I reply.
This has been my journey
It's all I have.

Grown Men

There are men
Who hold a woman's heart
Gently as a robin's egg
Tender as the moon alights
on a summer lake
Who hear the no
in uncertainty
And the yes
in dreamy wakefulness
Who see
their own heart's reflection
in the beauty
of their lover's Happiness

Raise a cheer for each
And etch their names
For eternity
In the chambers of your heart

Evolution

The ape knows:
It's the meat of the fruit
That sustains and refreshes.

But you,
Oh cultured Man,
Discard the fruit
After tasting the peel
Then wonder
Why you're not
Satisfied.

What Do I Want?

I want to fight with you
To argue politics
And religion
Passionately

I want to know
Everything
And understand
Not a damned thing

I want to disagree
About the meaning of a poem
Or the reason
Behind a painter's choice

I want to be surprised
By the depth of your knowledge
And the obtuse angle
Of your ideas

I want to hear music
From your lips
In a beat
I'd never dreamed

Then
I want to hold you
In laughter
In the dead of night
Grateful for your hunger

I want to taste
The sweetness of your fingertips
And the tangy saltiness
Of your thighs

I want to be awakened
By your dreams
And put to sleep
Beside your tender heartbeat

You
My darling
You
Are what I want.

Vanity

Son of Samael
Hear your lost love's call
Flee the tremulous grasp
of Eve's ravenous daughters
Bejeweled with vanity's trinkets
Distractions from Adam's
Tasteless ribs
Come to Lilith's chamber
and find your freedom
in her fingertips
Your ecstasy bathed
on the tip of her tongue
Flee the fraudulent rapture
and satisfy the depth of your longing
for Truth
in her fire.

Jaine

Swinging hope to hope
she holds on
for life
Fearless
and utterly afraid
of chasms unseen
yet remembered
from decades of falls
marked by psychic wounds
clearly visible
in only her mind's eye
Asking
what the hell
am I doing up here again
Seeing familiar trail marks
before her final drop
into unanswered questions.

My Wonderfully Transparent Poem

Your unexpected words echoed in my mind
Reverberated through bone and sinew, muscle and flesh.

Shockwaves of surprise pulsed from my heart
Tripped my internal balances
Set my fingertips ablaze,
Sent hunger pangs throbbing through my vagina.

Breathe, I told myself; just breathe.
Electricity filled the space between us, around us
Red light turned green without our notice
And then you walked away
  And away
    And away
      And away

Only to resurface with emotional amnesia
In an ice-encrusted, steel-edged email
Filled with smug, condescending professionalism
Leaving me to fight internal forest fires alone
Along a trail of exploding neural transformers
Hands burned by lava flows of tears
Throat sore from rivers of regurgitated unspoken rage
Shard sharp shreds of dead hope splintering out of my skin
Exploding behind social media poses
Threatening to travel the unseen psychic paths that bind us
To find your murderous soul and put it out of my final misery.

Release

Is it the curse
of every generation
to watch your dreams
come true for the next
And find a way to celebrate
their success
without bitterness and envy?

You are not mine to claim
The scion of another generation
Who could not have survived
The toxic birth pangs
Of mine.

What a bitter joy to know
we have created
a new world
where you can thrive
And be
the man we dreamed
into existence
but cannot hold.

Tango

My yesterdays
are your tomorrows
Shadows
Casting shimmering ghosts
as my faded memories
Clash
with your aspirational dreams
Leaving a trail
of dissatisfaction and ennui
Urging each of us to
Move along, move along
There's nothing here to see.

Waterfall = Cliff

Wordlessly
without touch
in your presence
dams break
metaphors flow
poetry bursts to life
Your eyes
your smile
ridiculous diversions
from the fiery soul
reaching me under
time and space
I will
survive you
again
my Muse
oh Son of Samael

Gratitude

How do you thank the waterfall
that appeared amid the desert
How do you explain that it gave you life
by doing nothing

Do you show it flowers
sprouting wildly from your heart
wild fruit growing from your fingertips
crimson rivers of hope coursing through your veins

Do you sing
midnight arias on the New moon
dance unrestrained
beneath the watchful gaze of the Full

How do you thank the waterfall
for transformation
when all it did was be
A waterfall.

Ah, Love

A gentle, sun-kissed stream
Meandering down verdant mountain slopes
Giving and receiving life
Bubbling, bounding, joyous

And

A lollygagging river
Dancing between flowered meadows
Slowly carving time out of ridges
Nurturing all it touches

Suddenly

Meet between walls
Of an immovable canyon
Constraining their waters
Forcing them to clash and rumble
Obliterating their individuality

Birthing

Passion
Fear
Love
Rage
Wonder
Confusion
Ecstasy
Awe

Until

Each finds its own appointed path
Beyond the canyon
Taking its reconstituted self
In new directions.

Blanks

Never heard the empty spaces
until I felt
the power of your gaze
in the depths of my soul
Awakened
by dissonant yearning
Calling out
Responding
Mourning the loss to come
Hungry
Oh lord
Hungry
To fill
The perpetual gap.

Valentine

Love is wasted on the young
An orchid in the hands of butchers
Unknowing, unfeeling of its fragility
Grasping at the flowers
Destroying the root
With the toxicity of ego

On 35

So sure
sure afraid
First consequences
yet to become evident
in their full extent
Dreams intact
Fissures silent
waiting
for forty
to send fractals
exploding through
your well-constructed
façade
of self definition
And uproot reality
from its concrete hold
on your daily life
So sure

Double takes

Mirror images
reflected
through prismatic time
bringing sons of memories
to the present
thru untouched photos
Uncorrected
to reflect
Reality

Falls

We met at the corner.
Red light.
Our eyes saw all,
Our hearts felt.

Life's music filled
Where logic failed.
We tangoed, waltzed, calypsoed,
Black-bottomed and jitterbugged.

Forever seemed like yesterday.
My heart lay finally bare, open,
Willing... Waiting.
Yellow light.

We parted friends.
Green light.

Mantelpiece

You hold my heart in this moment
Bare, open, trembling
Where will you leave it
Come morning.

Awakening

Oh to be young enough
to be seduced by mere beauty
without hunger
for a satisfying, well-turned
conversation the morning
After

Wobble

It's basic physics really
The wobble of the sun
indicates an unseen planet
pulling, tugging,
permanently claiming a piece
of your orbit.
And I thought
we were just dancing.

Divide

I've seen the road to madness
strewn with visions
of her ecstasy
in your arms
while my conscience screams
"Look away;
you have no rites here"
and my heart tears itself
apart
with pride that you
are that loyal man
who will nonetheless
No-ingly
walk away from
Me.

An Other Woman

He says
they have a non-exclusive
Arrangement

I know
I will be excluded
    on Valentines
    Thanksgiving
    at Christmas
    on New Years
    her birthday
    my birthday
    his birthday
    our friends' birthdays
    during vacations
    at dinner parties
    fundraisers
    weekend trips
    Mother's day
    Father's day
    Every day

I wonder
how she lays her heart
on the night stand beside him
every evening
Without seeing the missing pieces
he's auctioned off
throughout the day

Tenderhooks

How do I tell you
that I've seen
this film before
and you turn out to be
The villain
not the Hero
of your dreams.

Bridges you're travelling now
your rounded heels afire
will burn behind
and strand you
an isolated island
languishing amidst
other people's
dreams come true

Cornered by ambition
Silenced by self-proclaimed
Truth manipulated
To silence the empty
Seeing what you approve
Blind to reality
You destroy the champion within
Mistaking him for an enemy
Thwarting your salvation.

There is no happy ending
down this path my love
Turn back.

My Happy Poem

About the electric current
that erases my memory
churns my gut and stops my breath
when he's close enough to touch

About my dreams
of whispering ecstasy in his ear
and hearing his moans in mine
his touch igniting my soul

Whatever I may not have of him
This poem is mine forever
Reminding me that Love
Is not afraid of dry bones.

Burnt Sugar

I close my eyes
and dream of caramel
fingertips
along the fullness
of my lips

Sweetness of
nocturnal hungers
unmet

Fall

Based on the jazz composition
by Steve Moore

Letting go
Is the hardest gift
To give
Opening your heart
Beyond its own boundaries
Stretching your soul
'Til it tears apart
Not knowing if
It will ever repair
Or you will ever be
Whole again
Trusting a universe
Without proof
Of its trustworthiness
Only living
In the damnation of hope.

Light On Water II

Based on the painting by Anne Moorehouse

It ended magnificently, really.
A final explosion
illuminating the murky slough
that could have been the breeding ground
for something new
or the final resting place
of unfledged dreams.
Only the flapping of our determined Spirits
saved us to see it clearly
in the light of day.

Carnival

On	Off
Smile	Frown
He's in	He's out
He cares	He's careless
He loves me	He loves me not
Up	Down

Your friendship is a fun-house ride
without the fun.
An amusement park excursion
but I'm no longer amused.

I paid with loyalty, trust,
openness, vulnerability
What did I get in exchange?
A chance to throw up in public.

Bermuda

Call me Bermuda.
No, it's not my name.
That's who HE thinks I am:
An island in his storms of life
To be abandoned in my hurricanes.

Fraud

Bait - Private

You hold me like the world exists
only between our heartbeats
Universes collapse
if we part

We unwrap one another
word by word
wounds unwound
willingly softening

My spirit nestles
into childhood sense memory
of unencumbered safety
love unconditional

Switch - Public

The curtain rises
You sit beside me
Stiff
Your back a wall between me
And your history
Your hands clasped tightly
Between your knees

My speechless heart
records this moment
for the grief to come
When the cock refuses to crow
But your lips betray us both anyway

Collectors

One
Chasing between scented pines
Pounding through forest thick-
ets
Heartbeats a'thumping
Dashing hither thither
Following winged flashes
Reaching beyond boundaries
Recklessly tossing baited calls
Until it tires
Trapped

Two
Silent unrushed footsteps
Watch
Follow
Pause
Gauge
Resume
Trust extended
Captivated
Captured

Three
Quiet
Seated
Waiting
Measured breath
Belying Nothing
Steady single motion
Whispered network
Of half truths
Sprung
Taken

Results
The same
Always
Pinned
Beauty in stasis
Paraded over
  Champagne and caviar
  Coffee and cupcakes
  Cassis and cookies
Flattered for
  Little black cover
  Red-filigreed patterns
  Bright yellow dots
Book closed
Drawer shut
Until
The next one comes along.

Dissonance

I found
him
woven among
the poesy on each page
birthed by unloosed droplets
from my eyes and
stitched by filaments of tender awe
heartsick with the knowledge
the book was only borrowed
So I read slowly
lips forming the wisp of his name
fingers aching for his feel
holding him to my breast
Dream and Life entwined
until dawn brought
Light
and her sister
Truth
to erase the glimmer of
Hope's shadow.

Discombobulation

There is war
My heart declared it
Mind accepted the challenge
Body provided ammunition
Soul agreed to arbitrate
I cannot win
One part of me will damage the other
Irreparably
All will see bruised remains
None the source
Your eyes glaze over
Bored
Waiting for the next in line.

Extinguished

Butterfly lands in his open hand
tired from traversed canyons
wings tattered in gale-force winds
exhaustion rising steam-like from her heart.
Gently
deliberately
he closes his fist
until only the dust of memory
remains

Insomnia

I paint myself
onto his empty canvas
(with vivid dreams
dredged from nocturnal symphonies
only to find
his visual field
limited
to her pastels
his hearing
tuned
to her rhythms)
unable to quell
the gnawing in my spirit
that screams his name
at daybreak

Leavings

Just another falling leaf
Caught in the intrigue of
your peripheral vision
One moment
as you return
to gaze with longing
at the future
Unaware the heartache
of your back
now turned

Grief

Tears of the world
gather at the ocean's shores
murmuring sorrows
into each grain of sand
beneath the screech of
gulls diving to feast
on carcasses of dreams
fantasies built on
false memories
It's you I miss

Endings

Endings, in real life,
don't come in big waterfall splashes
They drip, instead,
moment by moment:
a word not spoken
a sigh without pleasure
a gaze unreturned.
And soon the river
has turned to stones
and all that's left is the
pronouncement
of last rights.

Deciduous

Did the crimson leaf know
even as summer vitality
coursed through its veins
what was to come?

Did the amber leaf shudder
even as it fluttered
in the first whisper
of June's breeze?

Did the golden leaf hear
the mournful note
even amidst April's
vivid song?

Did you feel
the chasm born
in the world
between our lips?

Ignition

Pathways blocked
Dreams held in remission
Expectations unimagined
Screams suppressed
What will come
Gone
Hearing restored
In empty space
Take me back to the source
Cleanse my synaptic pathways
Reboot

The Crimson Feather Trail

He locked her in
the utility closet of his soul
and fed her love poems
under the door
She used them for
seppuku
Crimson screaming
from the walls
"never let them take you
to a second location."

Shapeshifter

How exhausting it must be
to change your face
with each encounter
down to the flutter of your lashes

How fearful you must be
of the bubbling molten core within
lest it be seen
in all its raging, frightened glory

How horrible the acts
that sent you so deep
beneath the surface
of your own consciousness

How malevolent the souls
who provided
the bricks and mortar
to enclose your heart

How damned the perpetrators
who removed your Self
without psychic anesthesia
leaving pain your guiding force

How anguishing the stub
of referred existential pain
reminding you the wholeness
that once was

Yet still, beloved,
You
leak out
through the tip of a pen
uncontainable

Ah that the key were mine
to let you roam the world
natural untamed
without fetters

The earth liberated by your roar
set ablaze by the heat of your truth
quenched by the integrity of your vision
comforted by the strength of your vulnerability

Ah that the power were mine
to free the quaking child within
let flow the tears and screams
pent up behind these decades

Too late I came to see you clearly
confused by the mirror image
seduced by my own loneliness
blinded by projected primal colors

May you find the lighted path
out of your labyrinth
my beloved
beyond the shadows of time

Where you may see and claim
the identity of your true birth
setting aside the façades
you show the world

May you insist on full Existence
and this lifetime bring you the joy
of January's ambient sunlight
May you live.
May You live.
May YOU live.

The hobbling on an unbroken wing

refusing to take flight
The desperate cries for water
beside the clear and gently flowing stream

How did I not see you feeding
on the decay of my desperate grief
sucking the heat
from my writhing heart

Know this
I see you now
Clearly as against a cloudless sky
You will not play this game with me
Again.

Know this
I see you
Now.

Delusion

He has feelings for
her. They just don't include faith,
respect, or honor.

Lay-off

You wander through my dreams
A holographic projection
Speechless
Sightless
Focused ever forward
A shimmer promising everything/nothing
There/not there
Shadow against the rocks
I yearn to follow
You pass
I stay
There's work to do.

Self
seduction

The most dangerous lies
are the ones we tell ourselves
convinced that what others need
is the same as what we want
imposing our wreck-less fantasy
on their reality
and justifying it with a smirk
because we've done
what's right
(but for whom, dearest,
for whom)
then betraying our lie
by taking offense at
their thankless grumbling

Hope

Hope
You are the Master of the Universe.
Your whisper arouses ghosts of life in death.
Your dreams deceive and draw tomorrow's shadow in light.
Most sinister, you promise what you cannot deliver.

Destroyer of reality and reason.
Liar.

Dimensions

Standing before you
Bare,
I await recognition.
Sunlight filters through my pores
Reaching to caress you with my warmth.

Blinded by your self-made image of me
You walk past,
Acknowledge my shadow,
My specter,
Then curse the cold that is your world.

David

Beautiful apple
Luring starving hearts to bite
Poison at the core

Low T

He shoots mental blanks
Seedless, frothy ideas
Flashy and loud
With no chance of a future
Luring barren women
With promises
He has no agency
To keep.

Falling

Leaves passing time
Remind us
Letting go isn't an option
It's mandatory
For survival

Regeneration

Love

A howling wind
Tore out the old oak
By the roots
Left a gaping abyss
Jagged torn

Meadow screamed
in fruitless agony
each blade of grass trembling
empathetic fury
Helpless

Clouds amassed
drowned her with compassion
Sun screamed
scorched her tender bareness
Night sighed
blanketed her lonely grief

Time trembled
flora fauna inched forward
back
Time shuddered
forward forward forward
back
Time sighed
forward forward forward

Acorns cracked
rooted
tore her flesh
sprouted

Seasons change
Life gives
takes
gives again

life
love

Perspective

Blessed is the predator
who tears apart his prey
in full view of the herd
relishing every bite
and its reflected victory
giving full honor to his victim
by publicly glorying in his satisfaction
celebrating his own nature.

Cursed the hyena
who claims to entertain with laughter
while plotting, prowling
under night's cowardly cover
to tear apart the straggler's heart
before morning's light
exposes his nature
to all

Werd

Brained
drained
lamed
flayed
played
failed
railed
trailed
framed
gamed
blamed
Untamed

Grace

You drove me deep,
deep down
into the well
'til my pleading eyes
were out of your sight
and the wail of my spirit
beyond your hearing.
You did not know
the walls were made
of gold
and the sweet river
of Life
ran below.

Focus
(aka... Not What I Intended to Write!)

I asked the universe
to remind me
why my heart
shouldn't break apArt
And one by one
they marched back into
My Life
Reminders
with every hug
of the options
my Psyclops
never saw.

Turning Tides

Cleanse me
holy heartbeat of the sea
merge my melted dreams
into your drifting memory
spread your salt into my wounds
winnow within the welter of my soul
forgive the failings of this feeble human
heart humbly held fruitlessly
barren seed broken.

Undying Love

We stand
separated by the shimmer of
Time
Space
yours the sweet, carefree smile
of contentment

> *Love, you say*
> *is Action, not Feeling*
> *Taking out the trash*
> *changing the toilet roll*
> *cleaning out the fridge*
> *emptying the dishwater*
> *Serving one another*
> *moment-to-moment*

I awake with tears on my cheeks
grateful
you have not forgotten me
Aware of the irony
in walking away again
from my own Shadow

Kindle

How will poets write of love
When teardrops can no longer
Fall on paper?

The Soloist

Turns out I'm a soloist.
Open my songbook
And every tune is written in my key,
Arranged to please me
Performed my way.

When I tour
The only baggage I carry is my own
The only instrument I tune and polish belongs to me
Those who cannot be responsible for their own load
Those who would overload the orchestra
With their burdens
Are left behind

My performances
Are joyous, unencumbered events
Filled with appreciation for the moment
Built on interlocking notes of human experience
And building the foundation for tomorrow's laughter.

Finito

These are my poems
Of love and loss
Of aborted dreams
And lingering shadows

These are the deleted
nocturnal hopes
Of my youthful
Ambitions

Here on this lingual altar
In their minutial arrogance
Mocking the present
Daring hope to rise again
From the tomb
Of my heart

Enough already
Enough

Winter in July

The itch of spring's tingle
now faint sense memory
Music of summer's smile
a faded earworm
Nuanced beauty of fall's truth
another ending

Withered blooms
Fruit fallen
Reservoir of tears drained
Rage cooled
Heart iced
Mind silenced

I have reaped what I have sown
The fallow time has come
The Wait begins
Again

Blueberry Tea

nectar
sweet
drips
thru
veins
to
brain
'til
all
remains
is Art

Created using Adobe InDesign™

Internal text font: Candara Regular 12 pt
Internal title fonts: Apple Chancery and Candara Bold
Cover fonts: Trajan Pro and Apple Chancery

www.ingramcontent.com/pod-product-compliance
Lightning Source LLC
Chambersburg PA
CBHW031523270326
41930CB00006B/502